Keyboard Theory

BOOK ONE

DAVID KRAEHENBUEHL

with *Frances Clark*

and *Louise Goss*

©1978 by Summy-Birchard Music
division of Birch Tree Group Ltd.
Princeton, New Jersey U.S.A.
All rights reserved.   Printed in U.S.A.

ISBN 0-87487-115-8

1 2 3 4 5 6 7 8 9 10 11 12 13 14 15 16

Summy-Birchard Music
Princeton, New Jersey

Preface

The six books in the KEYBOARD THEORY series offer an imaginative new approach to theory designed to help piano students learn the fundamentals of music and traditional harmonic practice quickly, easily, musically. A carefully planned program of keyboard activities develops the student's skill in transposing, improvising accompaniments, harmonizing melodies in three and four parts, and composing in the smaller forms. Musical materials — folk tunes, themes from classical literature, original contemporary compositions — give the student experience with a variety of styles and idioms.

The goal of these books is understanding music; the keyboard is the means. Each new musical element is presented at the keyboard, explained in terms of the keyboard, then used extensively in keyboard activities. In this way, the student's understanding of music develops in his hands and in his ear.

In using these books, the teacher will find that some students may complete several numbered sections a week, while others may require more time. Whatever the pace, the only reasonable guide to weekly assignments is the student's *keyboard mastery* of the material.

Frances Clark
Princeton, New Jersey

Notes on Book One

MAJOR AND MINOR 5-FINGER PATTERNS

The student begins his study of keyboard theory with the simplest possible musical material, half steps and whole steps. These are used immediately to build major and minor 5-finger patterns, to transpose a piece to every major key, and to create compositions in small forms.

PERFECT 5THS

The student discovers that the top and bottom notes of a 5-finger pattern form a perfect 5th. Through experiments and creative activities to develop keyboard security in playing a 5th, he learns I and V of every major and minor key.

USING I, V AND VII TO ACCOMPANY 5-FINGER MELODIES

He confirms his knowledge of I and V in all keys by using them to accompany melodies. But instead of depending entirely on his ear, he learns how to use his hands at the keyboard to insure correct choices of I and V. In this way, his hands train his ear. When I and V are secure, the leading tone is presented as a half step below tonic and is added to the repertoire of accompaniment tones.

MAJOR KEYS

The remainder of Book One is an introduction to major keys. In a keyboard experiment the student transposes a piece to every major key, discovers that every major key has the same pattern of half steps and whole steps, and finds the black- and white-key pattern for every major key (in these books it is the keyboard pattern of a key that is stressed). After finding all the major keys, he works extensively with C, G, D, F and B♭ and learns to accompany melodies using I, V and VII of each key.

RHYTHM

Throughout the book there is specific instruction and drill in the rhythmic patterns ♪ ♩ ♪ and ♫♫ and in music written in ¢ and ⅜ meters.

We gratefully acknowledge permission to reprint melodies on the following pages:

French, German, 27; Mexican, Polish, 33; Brazilian, Mexican, 35; Polish, Austrian, 36; German, 48; from HARMONIZATION AT THE PIANO, copyright © 1962 by Arthur Frackenpohl.

American, 48; from PROMENADE ALL, copyright © 1947 by Janet E. Tobitt.

American, 45; from MORE SONGS TO GROW ON by Beatrice Landeck. Copyright © 1954 by Edward B. Marks Music Corporation.

British, German, 23; Dutch, 25; French, 35; both Czech, 43; from HARMONIZATION-TRANSPOSITION AT THE KEYBOARD by Alice M. Kern. Copyright © 1963 by Summy-Birchard Co.

American, Traditional, 18; Traditional, 25; both American, 31; Slovakian, 36; Folk Dance, Dutch, German, 45; from BIRCHARD MUSIC SERIES. Copyright © 1962 by Summy-Birchard Company.

Explanatory Note on Counting

For teachers who are unfamiliar with the approach to counting in the elementary LOOK AND LISTEN books, a word of explanation may prove helpful in understanding the rhythm pages of the KEYBOARD THEORY series.

In LOOK AND LISTEN, in order to relate the rhythm he *sees* to the pulse he *feels,* the student counts each note or rest for its own value rather than for its place in the measure.

For example, the student would count this pattern:

instead of:

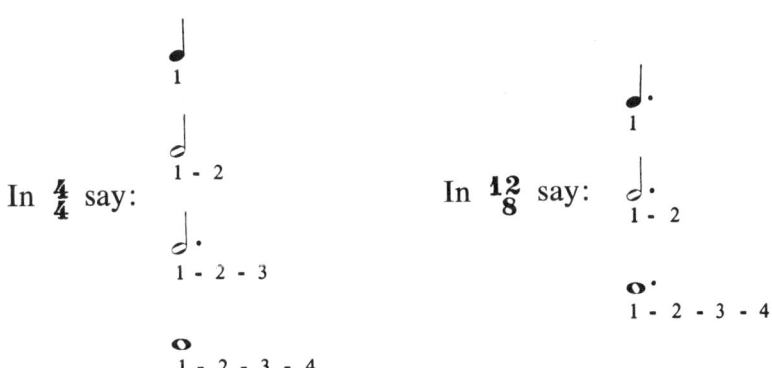

In KEYBOARD THEORY, this approach to counting continues. Each sign, in both simple and compound meters, is counted for its own value, no matter where it occurs.

Divided pulses, too, are counted for their own value, regardless of their position in the measure. Our way of counting divided pulses is based on verbalized breakdowns of the word "one" (since all such note values are a division of *one* pulse). Our choices are the ones we have found easiest for students to count aloud.

For example:

1 Half Steps and Whole Steps

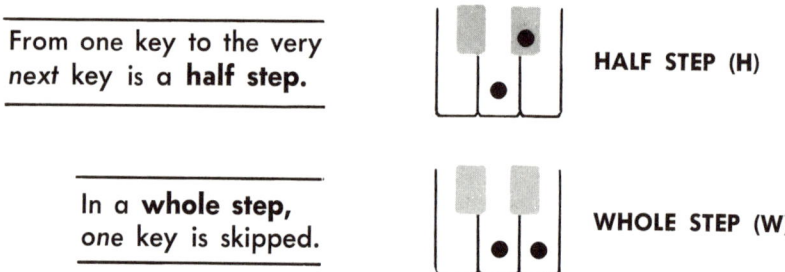

From one key to the very next key is a **half step**.   HALF STEP (H)

In a **whole step**, one key is skipped.   WHOLE STEP (W)

1. Play each of these intervals to decide whether it is a half step (**H**) or a whole step (**W**).
2. Then mark it **H** or **W**.

D♭	B	F	D♯	A♭	F	C	A♯	F♯	G
C	A	E♭	D	G	E	B♭	G♯	E	F♯
H	W	W	H	H	H	W	W	W	H

EXPERIMENT 1

HALF STEPS

Most half steps use *one white* key and *one black* key.

But there are *two* half steps that use *two white* keys.
Find and play them. Their names are:

__E__ to __F__   __B__ to __C__

Does a half step ever use *two black* keys? *Circle answer* YES **NO**

WHOLE STEPS

How many *different* whole steps can you find that use:

two white keys? __5__   two black keys? __3__

one white key and one black key? __2__

2 Using Half Steps and Whole Steps to Make Music

> Tones a half step or whole step apart are called **neighbor tones.**

Neighbor tones are often used to decorate a theme like this one.

THEME

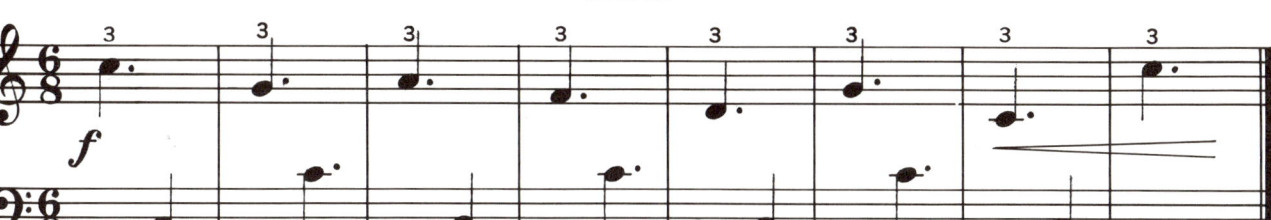

You can make a set of variations on this theme by decorating each **RH** note with neighbor tones. Here's one way:

VARIATION 1

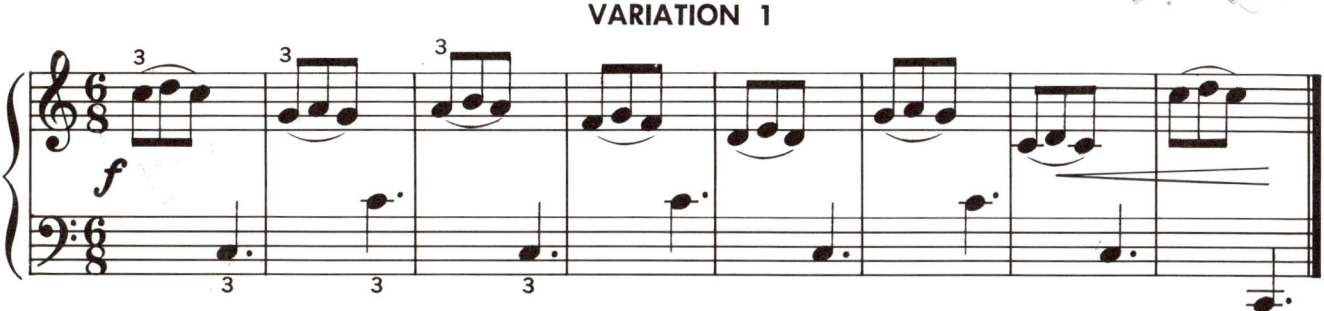

In *Variation 1*, each **RH** note is decorated by playing the theme tone, a neighbor tone, then the theme tone again, using the rhythm ♪♪♪ .

Are the neighbor tones a half step or whole step *above* the theme tones?

Circle answer
(H) W

Here are two other ways to decorate this theme.
Complete each variation with the decorating figure given.

VARIATION 2   **VARIATION 3**

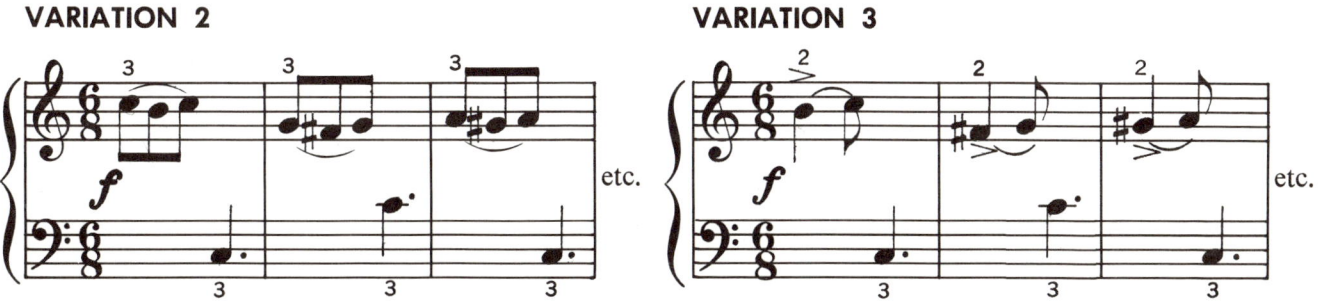

Now play the entire piece — the theme and all three variations.

5

3 Major 5-Finger Patterns

You can build a major 5-finger pattern beginning on any note. The note you begin on is called the "keynote."

To build a **major 5-finger pattern,** begin on the keynote and play *up* the keyboard, following the pattern:
W W H W

Each note in a 5-finger pattern is called a "degree."

The keynote is degree I. The highest note is degree __V__.

In a major 5-finger pattern there is just *one* half step.

Circle the half step in the 5-finger pattern above.

It is between degrees __III__ and __IV__.

On these keyboards, mark the keys that make a major 5-finger pattern up from each keynote.

Mark ⌢ to show the half steps.

(The first keyboard is marked to show you how.)

D MAJOR 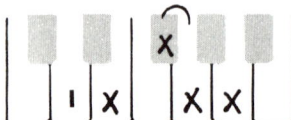   G MAJOR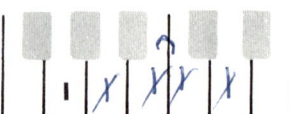

E MAJOR 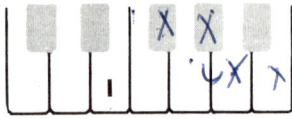   F MAJOR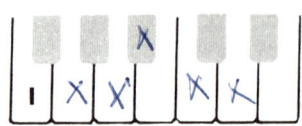

Which of these major 5-finger patterns use:
- one black key? __D__ __F__
- two black keys? __E__
- no black keys? __G__

EXPERIMENT 2

DECISION

In *Decision*, both hands are in the C-major 5-finger pattern.

Play the piece; then look at your hands on the keyboard.

In both hands, the half step is just *above* finger 3.

You can play *Decision* in any major 5-finger pattern.

1. Find the major 5-finger pattern beginning on each keynote.
2. Play *Decision* in that major 5-finger pattern.
3. Under **LEFT HAND** and **RIGHT HAND**, circle the numbers of the fingers that played *black* keys.

5-FINGER PATTERN	LEFT HAND	RIGHT HAND
C♯ Major	⑤ ④ 3 ② ①	① ② 3 ④ ⑤
D Major	5 4 ③ 2 1	1 2 ③ 4 5
E♭ Major	⑤ 4 3 ② ①	① 2 3 ④ ⑤
E Major	5 ④ 3 ② 1	1 ② ③ 4 5
F Major	5 4 3 ② 1	1 2 3 ④ 5
F♯ Major	⑤ ④ 3 2 ①	① 2 3 4 ⑤
G Major	5 4 3 2 1	1 2 3 4 5
A♭ Major	⑤ ④ 3 2 ①	① 2 3 4 5
A Major	5 4 ③ 2 1	1 2 ③ 4 5
B♭ Major	⑤ 4 3 ② 1	① 2 3 4 5
B Major	5 ④ 3 2 ①	1 ② ③ 4 ⑤

4 Using Major 5-Finger Patterns to Make Music

TRANSPOSING

When you finished the experiment on page 7, you had "transposed" *Decision* to all the major 5-finger patterns.

> **Transposing** means playing a musical idea exactly the same, but beginning on a *higher* or *lower* key.

Here is a musical idea to transpose.

1. Play *Marching* as written; then look at your hand on the keyboard. It is in the __D__ major 5-finger pattern.

2. Find the notes of the F-major 5-finger pattern.
3. Now transpose *Marching* to F major.

THREE-PART PLAN: AA'A

To make *Marching* into a longer piece, play it three times:
first in D major,
then transposed to F major,
finally in D major again.

This longer piece uses the same idea three times, so we could use the letters **AAA** to show the plan.

But because the middle section is transposed to a different key, **AA'A** shows the plan better.

Now play *Marching* following each of these three key plans:

D C D   D E D   D G D

Do the letters **AA'A** show the plan for each of these pieces?   YES   NO

Here are two other musical ideas to make into longer pieces by transposing.

1. Play the piece, following each key plan listed.
2. Circle the key plan you like best.

BEAR DANCE

KEY PLANS: F A F   F C F   F D F

INVENTION

KEY PLANS: G D G   G E G   G A G

OPUS 1

Now you can make your own pieces in major 5-finger patterns.

1. Decide what your piece will be about — running, sleeping, riding a bike, swinging in a hammock, or whatever you like.
2. Put your **RH**, **LH**, or both hands on the major 5-finger pattern you want to use.
3. Make a musical idea for your piece.
4. If you want to make your idea into a longer piece, transpose it to other major 5-finger patterns.

   Hint: A piece usually sounds more complete if the first and last parts are in the same key.

THREE-PART PLAN: ABA

Another way to make a piece of music is to compose one idea, then a completely *different* idea, and put them together, like this:

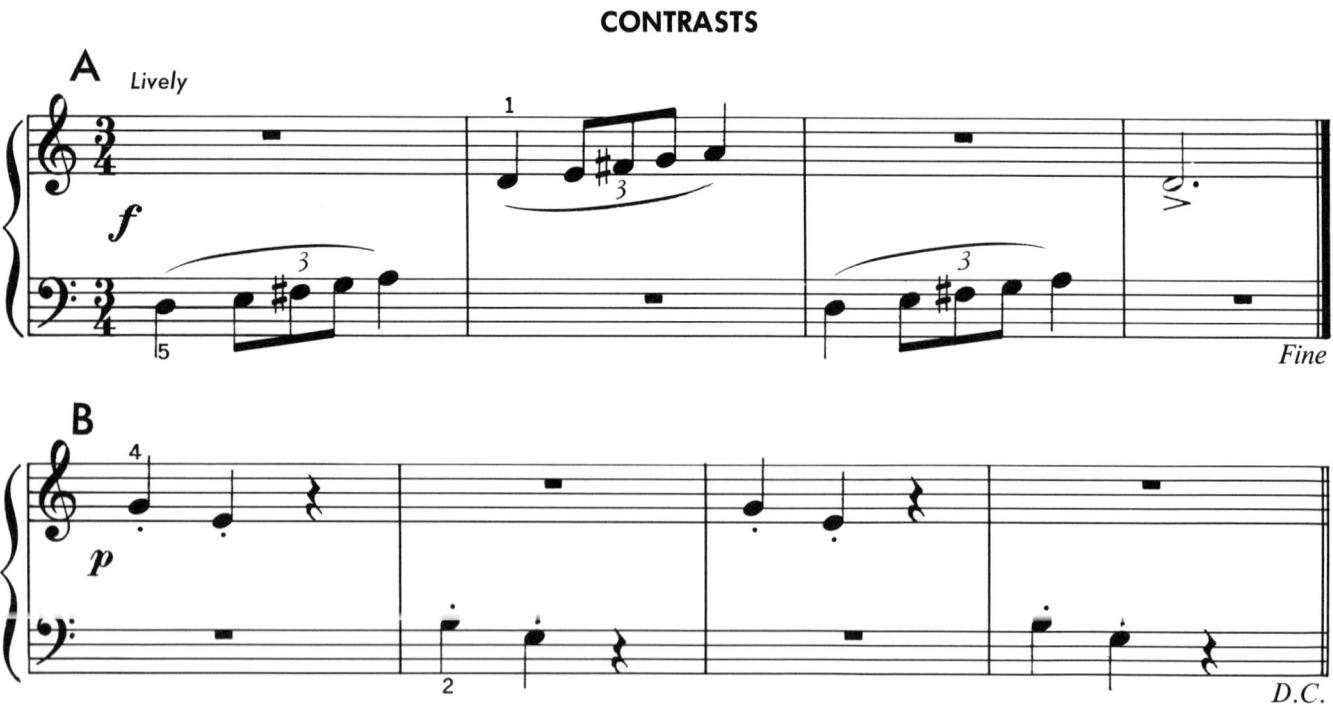

When a piece uses more than one idea, we need a new letter to show each new idea.

We call the first idea **A**, the next idea **B**, and so on.

Since the middle part of *Contrasts* is completely different from the first and last parts, the letters **ABA** show the plan.

Study *Contrasts* to see exactly *how* **B** is different from **A**.

Each measure of **A** goes up.	Each measure of **B** goes _____.
A is loud.	**B** is _____.
A is legato.	**B** is _____.
A moves mainly stepwise.	**B** moves mainly in skips.
A uses three kinds of notes:	**B** uses only one kind of note:
♩ ♫♪ ♩.	_____
A uses *all* the notes of the D-major 5-finger pattern.	**B** uses *only* degrees ___ and ___ of the D-major pattern.

Here are three ideas to use as the **A** parts for **ABA** pieces.

1. Play the **A** part and study it carefully, considering:

    loud or soft
    legato or staccato
    stepwise motion or skipwise motion
    note values
    which notes of the 5-finger pattern are used

2. Using the same 5-finger pattern, make a **B** part that is as different as possible from **A**.

3. Put the **A** part and your **B** part together to make an **ABA** piece.

OPUS 2

Now make your own piece using an **ABA** plan.

1. Think of two very different ideas — running and resting, jumping and sliding, gay and gloomy, or whatever you like.

2. Then put your **RH**, **LH**, or both hands on the major 5-finger pattern you want to use.

3. Make a musical idea for each part of your piece.

4. Then put them together, using the first idea, then the second idea, and finally the first idea again.

5 Accompanying Major 5-Finger Patterns

You can accompany any melody in a 5-finger pattern with the *lowest* and *highest* notes of that pattern, like this:

PARADE

Make a **LH** accompaniment for each of these melodies.

1. Play the melody and decide what 5-finger pattern it uses.
2. Play the melody again, accompanying it with the *lowest* and *highest* notes of the pattern.

STAMP DANCE

Now transpose *Stamp Dance* and your accompaniment to E major.

SWIRLING FOG

Now transpose *Swirling Fog* and your accompaniment to A major.

WALTZ

Now transpose *Waltz* and your accompaniment to F major.

6 Minor 5-Finger Patterns

> **Minor 5-finger patterns** are exactly like major, except for degree **III**.
>
> In *minor,* degree **III** is a *half step lower* than in major.

1. On the piano, find a C-major 5-finger pattern in each hand.
2. Now move the 3rd finger of each hand *down a half step.*

    In both hands, the half step is just *below* finger _____.

So, to make a major 5-finger pattern minor, all you need to do is move your 3rd finger *down a half step.*

Here are three melodies in major 5-finger patterns.

1. Play them as written.
2. Then move your 3rd finger *down a half step* and play them in minor.

    Listen to the difference in sound!

DOWN THE FIELD

TROLLING

CLOG WALTZ

Now play each melody in *minor* again, accompanying it with the lowest and highest notes of the pattern.

7 Parallel Major and Minor Patterns

Five-finger patterns that have the *same keynote* are called **parallel**.

INVENTION

Play *Invention;* then look at your hands on the keyboard.

    Both hands are in the _____ major 5-finger pattern.

    In each hand, the half step is just *above* finger _____.

To play *Invention* in the *parallel minor pattern,* all you need to do is move your 3rd finger *down a half step.*

Play *Invention* in the parallel minor; then look at your hands.
    In each hand, the half step is just *below* finger _____.

Now transpose *Invention* to D, and play it in each of these two key plans:

    D MAJOR - D MINOR - D MAJOR

    D MINOR - D MAJOR - D MINOR

    Do both key plans use parallel major and minor keys?   YES   NO

    Do the letters **AA'A** show the plan of both pieces?   YES   NO

EXPERIMENT 3

All the pieces on pages 8-12 use *major* 5-finger patterns.

Play each piece again, but this time in the *parallel minor* pattern.

    Remember, all you need to do to change a major pattern to minor is move finger 3 *down a half step.*

8 Using Major and Minor Patterns to Make Music

Here is a piece that uses the ____ minor 5-finger pattern.

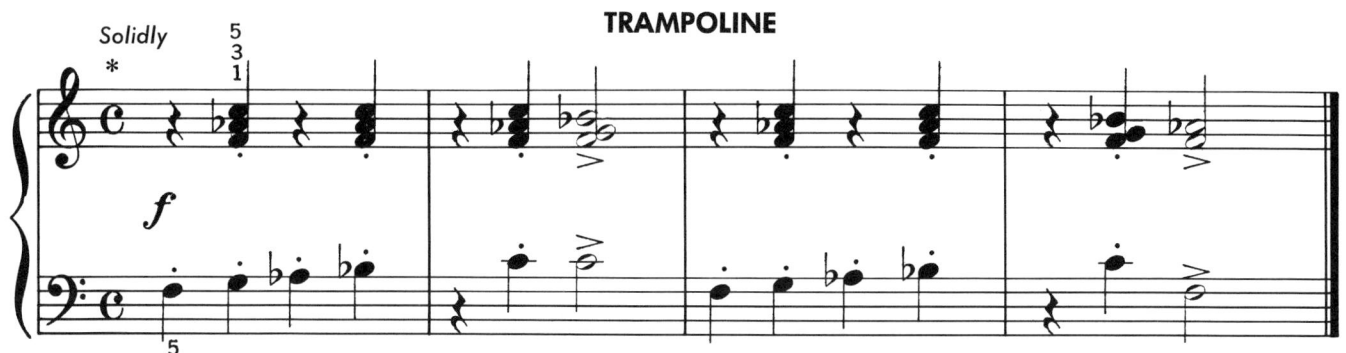

Here are some ways to develop *Trampoline* into a longer piece:

1. Play *Trampoline* in minor, then in parallel major, then in minor again.

    Write your key plan here: ____ MINOR ____ MAJOR ____ MINOR

2. Play *Trampoline* in minor, then transpose it to a *different* minor key, then play it in the original minor again.

    Write your key plan here: ____ MINOR ____ MINOR ____ MINOR

3. Play *Trampoline* in minor, then transpose it to some other *major* key (*not* the parallel major), then play it in the original minor again.

    Write your key plan here: ____ MINOR ____ MAJOR ____ MINOR

OPUS 3

Now make a piece of your own using parallel major and minor patterns.

1. Decide what your piece will be about.

2. Put both hands on the major 5-finger pattern you want to use.

3. Make a musical idea for your piece and play it in each of these two key plans:

    MAJOR - MINOR - MAJOR   MINOR - MAJOR - MINOR

    Do the letters **AA'A** show the plan of both pieces?   YES   NO

* **C** is simply another sign for $\frac{4}{4}$

15

9 Perfect 5ths

The interval between degrees **I** and **V** in a major 5-finger pattern is a **perfect 5th (P5)**.

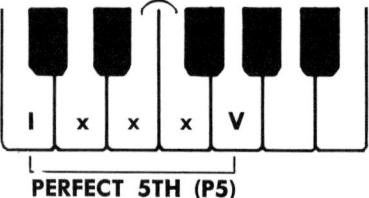

PERFECT 5TH (P5)

FINDING P5's WITH LH

1. Put **LH** finger 5 on the keynote (marked **I**); then play *up* a major 5-finger pattern.
   Be sure the half step is just *above* finger 3.
2. Play the **P5** (**I** and **V**).
3. Mark **V** on the highest note of the pattern.

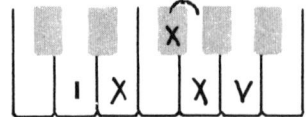  

FINDING P5's WITH RH

1. Put **RH** finger 5 on the key marked **V**; then play *down* a major 5-finger pattern.
   Be sure the half step is just *above* finger 3.
2. Play the **P5** (**I** and **V**).
3. Mark **I** on the keynote of the pattern.

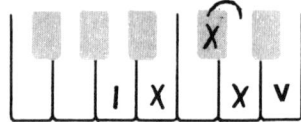 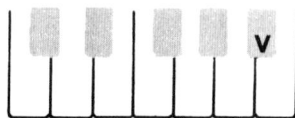 

 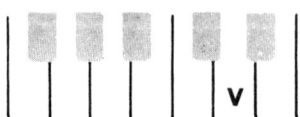 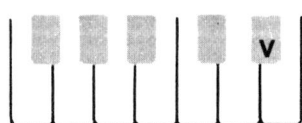

EXPERIMENT 4

Most **P5**'s use *two black* keys or *two white* keys.

But there are *two* **P5**'s that use *one black* key and *one white* key.

To find them, fill in the chart below.

1. Put your **RH** thumb on the lower note of each **P5**.
   If it is white, mark it *W;* if it is black, mark it *B*.

2. Play up the major 5-finger pattern to find the **P5** above.
   If it is white, mark it *W;* if it is black, mark it *B*.

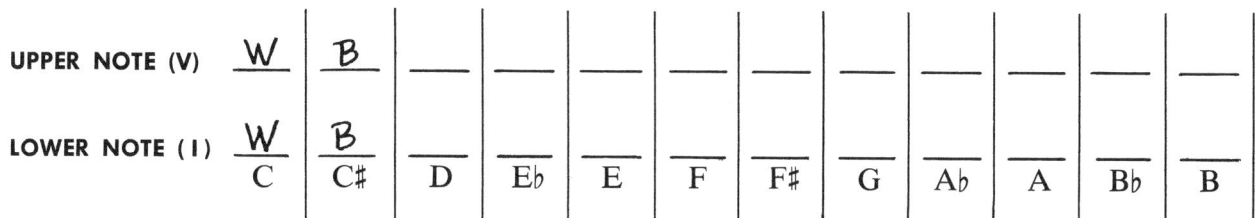

	C	C#	D	Eb	E	F	F#	G	Ab	A	Bb	B
UPPER NOTE (V)	W	B										
LOWER NOTE (I)	W	B										

The two **P5**'s that use *one black* key and *one white* key are:

Bb to _____   _____ to F#

With **LH** play a **P5** *above* each note.

With **RH** play a **P5** *below* each note.

With both hands, find and play all the **P5**'s that use:

two white keys

two black keys

one white key and *one black* key

17

10 Using Perfect 5ths to Make Music

Here are some familiar melodies for you to play in perfect 5ths.

WITH LH

Play *Yankee Doodle,* adding a **P5** *above* each melody note.
(Some of the 5ths are written in to get you started.)

YANKEE DOODLE

WITH RH

Play *Good King Wenceslas* and *Pierrot,* adding a **P5** *below* each melody note.
(Some of the 5ths are written in to get you started.)

GOOD KING WENCESLAS

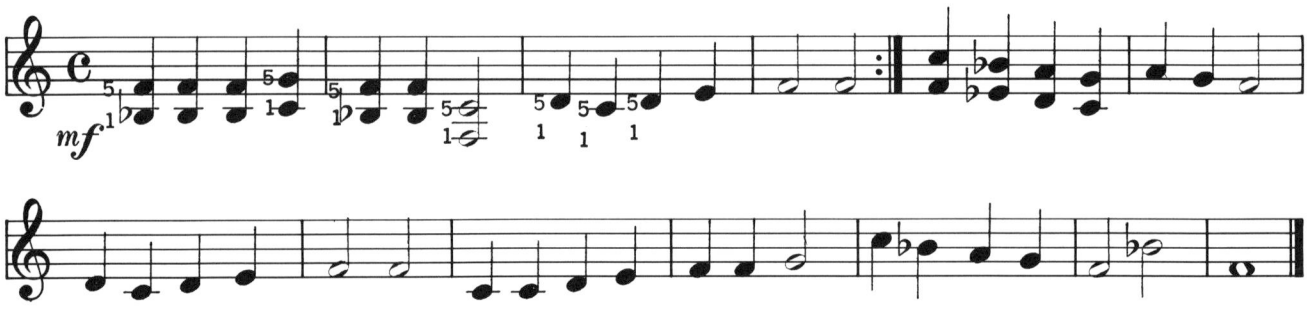

PIERROT

WITH BOTH HANDS

Play *Temple Lagoon* and *Perfect Blues,* adding a **P5**:

below each **RH** note,
above each **LH** note.

TEMPLE LAGOON

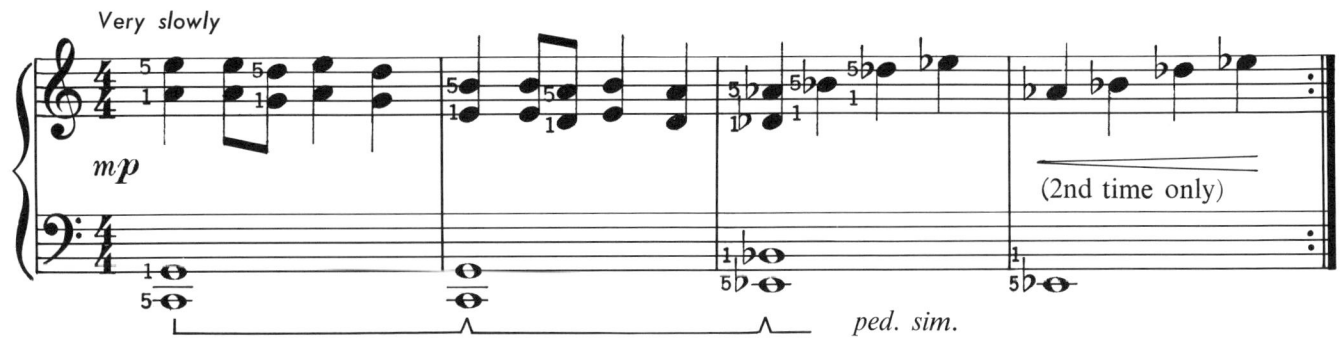

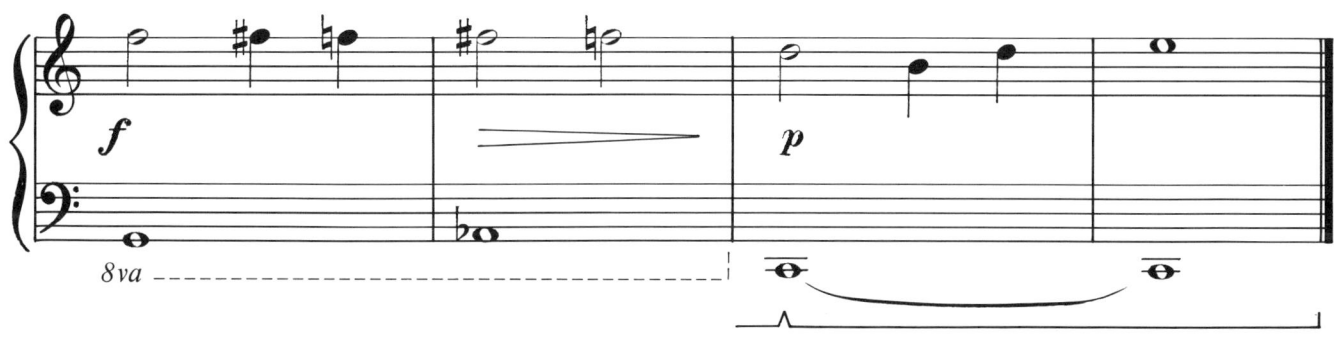

PERFECT BLUES

11 Perfect 5ths: Blocked and Broken

When the notes of a P5 are played *at the same time,* the 5th is called **blocked.**

Do all the pieces on pages 17-19 use *blocked* 5ths?　　**YES　　NO**

When the notes of a P5 are played *one after the other,* the 5th is called **broken.**

Rocking the Boat uses both blocked and broken 5ths.

Which hand plays *broken* 5ths?　　**LH　　RH**

Which hand plays *blocked* 5ths?　　**LH　　RH**

ROCKING THE BOAT

OPUS 4

Now make a piece of your own using perfect 5ths. The 5ths can be blocked, broken, or both.

1. Decide what you want your piece to be about — clouds, bells, or whatever you like.

2. Using both hands, try various combinations of 5ths on the piano until you find a musical idea for your piece.

12 Triad and Non-Triad Tones

Degrees **I**, **III** and **V** of any 5-finger pattern form a "triad."

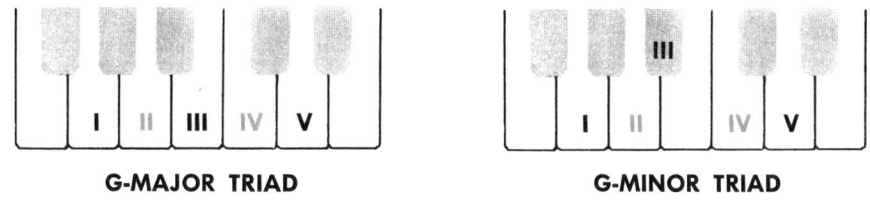

G-MAJOR TRIAD   **G-MINOR TRIAD**

In a *major* 5-finger pattern, they form a *major* triad.

In a *minor* 5-finger pattern, they form a *minor* triad.

> Because degrees **I**, **III** and **V** form a triad, they are called **triad tones.**

Which two degrees are *not* part of the triad? _____ and _____

> Degrees **II** and **IV** are called **non-triad tones.**

Ramble is in the E-major 5-finger pattern. Before playing:

1. Write the names of the notes in the E-major triad.
2. Mark + over the measures that use *non*-triad tones.

Musing is in the D-minor 5-finger pattern. Before playing:

1. Write the names of the notes in the D-minor triad.
2. Mark + over the measures that use *mostly non*-triad tones.

13 Using Tonic and Dominant Tones as Accompaniments

In a 5-finger pattern:
   degree **I** is called **tonic**;
   degree **V** is called **dominant**.

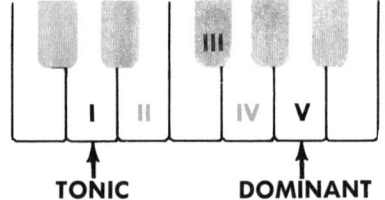

Because tonic (**I**) and dominant (**V**) are the two most important tones in a 5-finger pattern, they are often used to accompany a melody written in that pattern.

Here are *Ramble* and *Musing* again, this time accompanied with tonic and dominant.

RAMBLE

Ramble is in _____ major. Tonic (**I**) is _____ ; dominant (**V**) is _____ .

The accompaniment is made entirely of these two notes.

   Mark **I** above each tonic; mark **V** above each dominant.

MUSING

Musing is in _____ minor. Tonic (**I**) is _____ ; dominant (**V**) is _____ .

The accompaniment is made entirely of these two notes.

   Mark **I** above each tonic; mark **V** above each dominant.

Look at the accompaniments on page 22 again. Notice that:

    in measures made mostly of *triad* tones, the **LH** plays degree ____;

    in measures made mostly of *non*-triad tones, the **LH** plays degree ____.

When you can play each of the following melodies easily, make a **LH** accompaniment for it, using tonic and dominant tones.

1. Mark **V** under measures made mostly of *non*-triad tones.

2. Put your **RH** on the 5-finger pattern.
   Put your **LH** an octave lower:
       finger 5 on tonic,
       thumb on dominant.

3. Accompany the melody:
       use dominant where you marked **V**,
       use tonic everywhere else.

*When the melody begins with an upbeat, do not accompany the upbeat, but begin your accompaniment on the first full measure.

14 Perfect 4ths

From tonic (I) *up* to dominant (V) is a **P5**.

From tonic (I) *down* to dominant (V) is a **P4**.

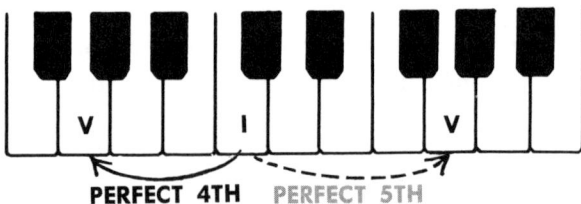

A **P4** is made by taking the upper note of a **P5** and putting it *below* the lower note.

When the notes of an interval are rearranged so there is a new *lower* note, the new interval is called an "inversion."

A **P4** is an **inversion** of a **P5**.

On each of the keyboards below, mark the key a **P5** *above* and a **P4** *below* each checked key.

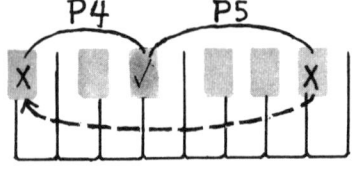 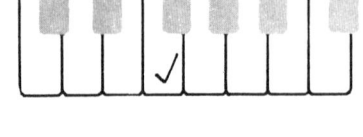 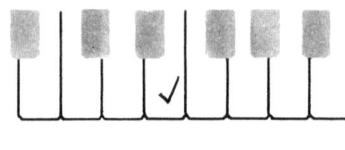

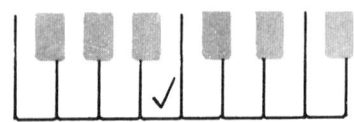  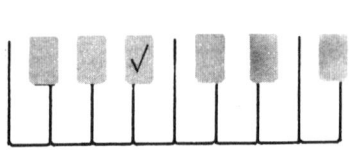

Is each **P4** an inversion of the **P5**?   YES   NO

EXPERIMENT 5

Like **P5**'s most **P4**'s use *two white* keys or *two black* keys.
But there are *two* **P4**'s that use *one white* key and *one black* key.

To find them, play from C up to C:
    add a **P5** *above* each **RH** note,
    add a **P4** *below* each **LH** note.

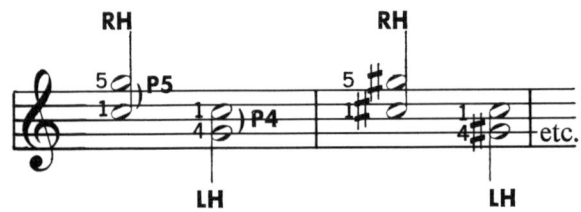

The two **P4**'s that use *one white* key and *one black* key are:

    _____ to B♭   F♯ to _____

15 Using Perfect 4ths to Accompany Melodies

As you know, any melody in a 5-finger pattern can be accompanied with:

tonic (**I**) for measures made mostly of *triad* tones;

dominant (**V**) for measures made mostly of *non*-triad tones.

The dominant is a **P5** *above* tonic,
or a **P4** *below* tonic.

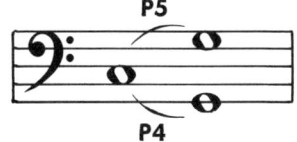

The dominant a **P4** *below* tonic is usually used in accompaniments.

For example:

Gaily — Dutch

Here is a melody to accompany with tonic and dominant.

1. Mark **V** under measures made mostly of *non*-triad tones.

2. Put your **RH** on the 5-finger pattern.
   Put your **LH** an octave lower:
   thumb on tonic,
   finger 4 on the dominant *below* tonic.

3. Accompany the melody:
   use the dominant *below* tonic where you marked **V**;
   use tonic everywhere else.

Allegro — Traditional

*When a measure has an equal number of triad and non-triad tones, accompany it with
I if the triad tones last longer, **V** if the non-triad tones last longer.

16 Counting 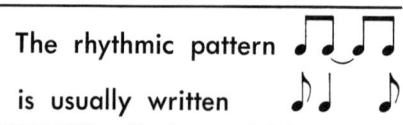 When ♩ Is the Sign for One Pulse*

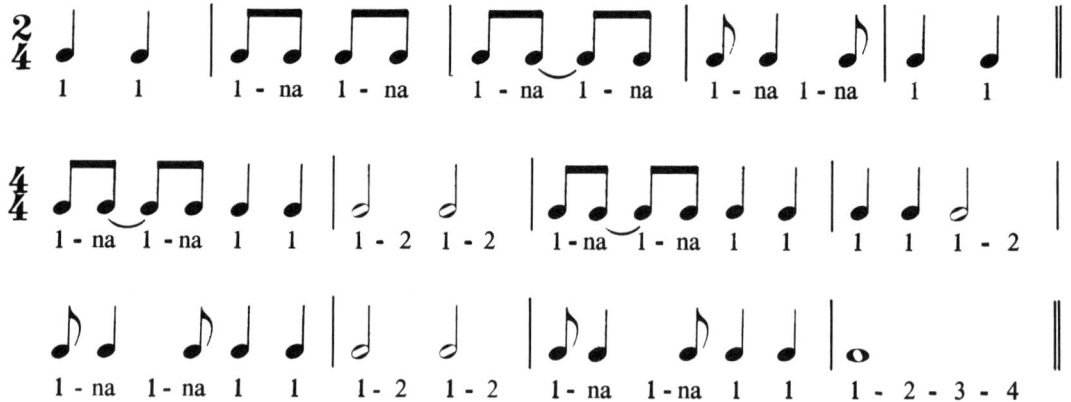

To learn this new rhythmic pattern:
1. Point to the notes and count.
2. Tap and count.

Here are two melodies using this new rhythmic pattern.
Before playing, tap and count.

When you can play each melody *easily and securely,* make a **LH** accompaniment for it (follow the instructions on page 25).

*See Explanatory Note (page 3) for explanation of counting.

17 Using the Leading Tone in Accompaniments

> The **leading tone (LT)** is the note a *half step below tonic*.

When you make an accompaniment, you can use the *leading tone* instead of the dominant to accompany *non*-triad measures.

Using Dominant

Using Leading Tone

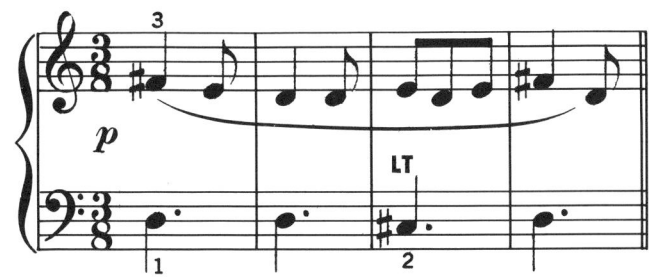

Here are two melodies to accompany with tonic and leading tone.

1. Mark **LT** under measures made mostly of *non*-triad tones.

2. Put your **LH** an octave below your **RH**:
    thumb on tonic,
    finger 2 on leading tone (half step below tonic).

3. Accompany the melody:
    use leading tone where you marked **LT**,
    use tonic everywhere else.

27

18 Major Keys

> A **major key** is a set of tones related to a keynote (tonic) in a special way.

This piece has the tonic C and uses all the notes in the key of C major.

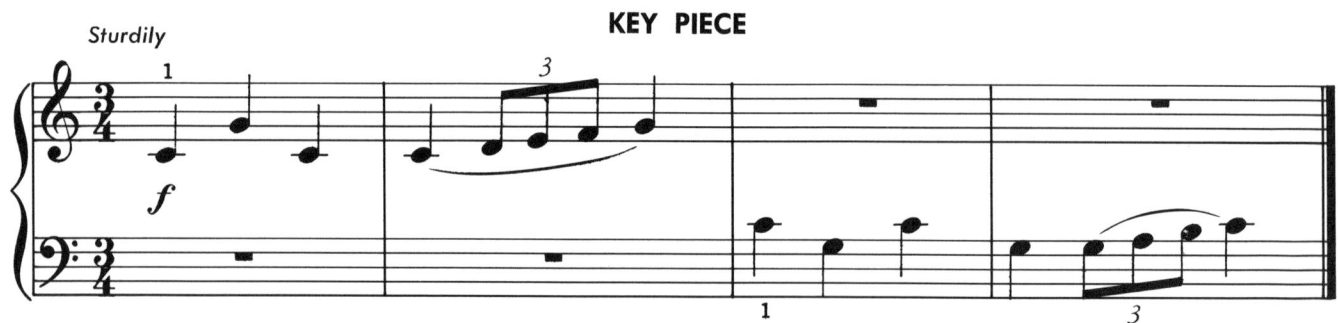

The notes of a major key are divided into two parts:

the **P5** *from* **I** *up to* **V**

    These notes form a major 5-finger pattern.

    Mark **x** on the keys your **RH** played in *Key Piece*.

        The half step is just *above* finger_____.

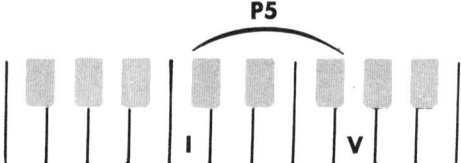

the **P4** *from* **V** *up to* **I**

    Mark **x** on the keys your **LH** played in *Key Piece*.

        The half step is just *below* finger_____.

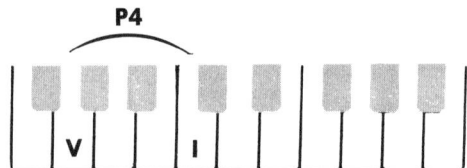

When the notes of a major key are written *in order* from tonic to the tonic an octave higher, they form a "scale."

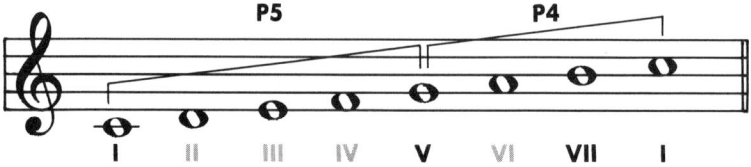

Each note of the scale has a "degree number."

    Tonic is **I** ; dominant is _____ ; leading tone is _____ .

Mark ⌒ to show the two half steps in the scale above.

    They are between degrees **III** and _____ , and degrees _____ and **I**.

EXPERIMENT 6

Use *Key Piece* on page 28 to find the notes of all the major keys.

1. Put both thumbs on the tonic nearest the middle of the piano:
   RH over the major 5-finger pattern from **I** up to **V**,
   LH over the notes from **I** down to **V**.
   (Be sure the half step is between fingers 1 and 2.)

2. Play *Key Piece,* transposed to each major key.
   Did it sound the same, except higher or lower?

3. Under **LEFT HAND** and **RIGHT HAND**, circle the numbers of the fingers that played *black* keys.

MAJOR KEY	LEFT HAND				RIGHT HAND			
C Major	4	3	2	(1)	2	3	4	5
	V		I				V	
C♯ Major	④	③	2	⑴	②	3	④	⑤
D Major	4	3	2	(1)	2	3	4	5
E♭ Major	4	3	2	(1)	2	3	4	5
E Major	4	3	2	(1)	2	3	4	5
F Major	4	3	2	(1)	2	3	4	5
F♯ Major	4	3	2	(1)	2	3	4	5
G Major	4	3	2	(1)	2	3	4	5
A♭ Major	4	3	2	(1)	2	3	4	5
A Major	4	3	2	(1)	2	3	4	5
B♭ Major	4	3	2	(1)	2	3	4	5
B Major	4	3	2	(1)	2	3	4	5

19 The Key of C Major

As you already know, the key of C major uses only *white* keys.

On this keyboard, mark x on the keys to complete C major.

Did you mark any black keys?   YES   NO

Letter names for three important notes in C major are:

tonic _____   dominant _____   leading tone _____ (half step below tonic)

> The triad built on the tonic tone is called the **tonic triad.**

In C major, tonic is _____ .

So the tones of the tonic triad are _____ _____ _____ .
                                                 I   III   V

> All the other tones in a key are called **non-tonic tones.**

In C major, the *non*-tonic tones are _____ _____ _____ _____ .

To accompany melodies in C major, use:

tonic (I) for measures made mostly of tones in the *tonic* triad,

dominant (V) for measures made mostly of *non-tonic* tones.

For example:

20 Accompanying Melodies in C Major

When you can play each of these melodies easily, make a **LH** accompaniment for it.

1. Mark **V** under measures made mostly of *non*-tonic tones.

2. Put your **LH** an octave below your **RH**:
    thumb on tonic,
    finger 4 on the dominant *below* tonic.

3. Accompany the melody:
    use dominant where you marked **V**,
    use tonic everywhere else.

FOLK DANCE

21 The Key of G Major

Look back at the experiment on page 29 and study the key of G major.

On this keyboard, mark the keys to complete G major.

G major uses one black key, F♯.

F♯ is the **TOP**/**BOTTOM** key in the groups of **TWO**/**THREE** black keys.

G major uses all the white keys in the octave except _____.

Because music in the key of G major uses one sharp, the F♯ is shown at the beginning of each line.

> Sharps or flats at the beginning of a line are called the **key signature**.

March is in the key of G major. We know it is G major because:

it ends on the tonic _____; the key signature is one sharp _____.

In the music, circle all the notes you will play on black keys.

On the piano, find all the F♯'s you will play in this piece.

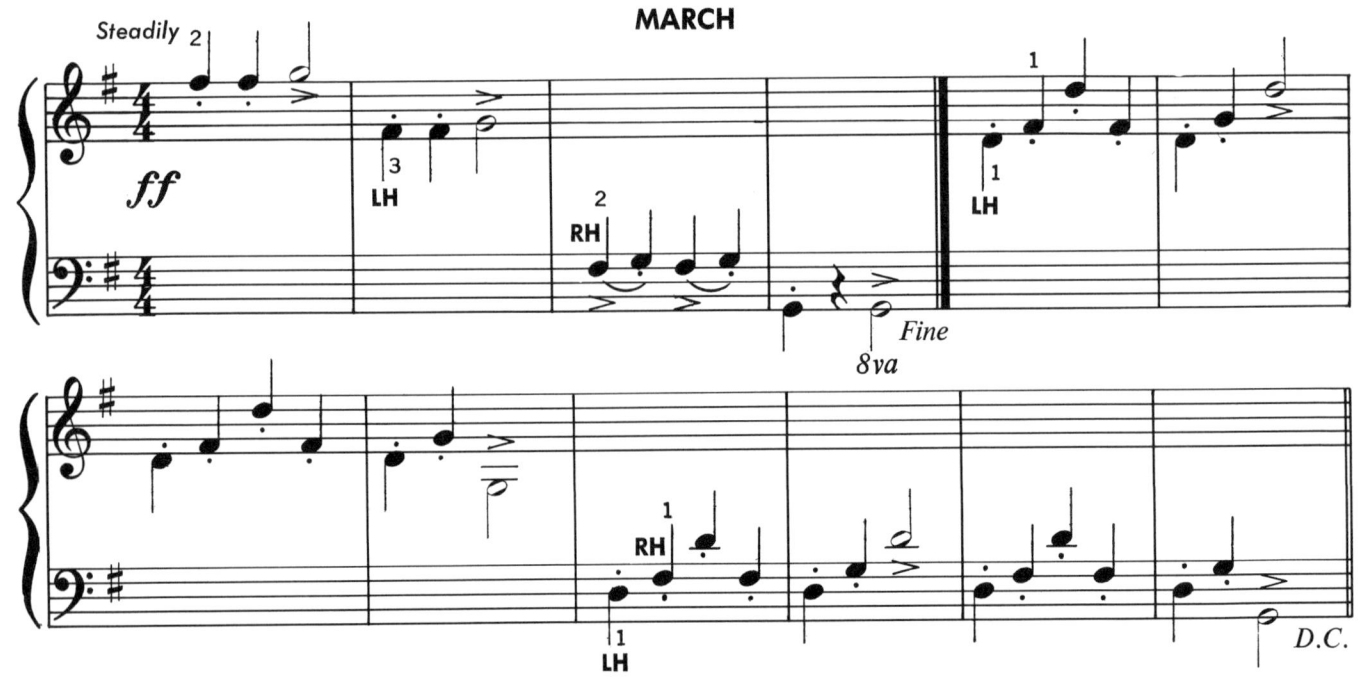

This piece uses only three important notes in G major:

tonic (I) _____   dominant (V) _____   the only black key _____.

Since the only black key is a half step below tonic, it is the leading tone.

22 Accompanying Melodies in G Major

In G major the tones of the tonic triad are ____ ____ ____ ;

the *non*-tonic tones are ____ ____ ____ ____ .

When you can play each melody easily, make a **LH** accompaniment for it (follow the instructions on page 31).

As you know, leading tone (**LT**) can be used instead of dominant (**V**) to accompany measures made mostly of non-tonic tones.

In G major, **LT** is ____ (half step below tonic).

Accompany the melodies on this page again, but this time:
use **LT** to accompany the *non*-tonic measures;
use tonic everywhere else.

23 The Key of D Major

Look back at the experiment on page 29 and study the key of D major.

On this keyboard, mark
the keys to complete D major.

D major uses two black keys, F♯ and C♯.

They are the **TOP / BOTTOM** keys in the groups of black keys.

D major uses all the white keys in the octave except _____ and _____.

Kangaroos is in the key of D major. We know it is D major because:

it ends on the tonic _____ ; the key signature is two sharps _____ and _____.

In the music, circle all the notes you will play on black keys.

On the piano, find all the F♯'s and C♯'s you will play in this piece.

KANGAROOS

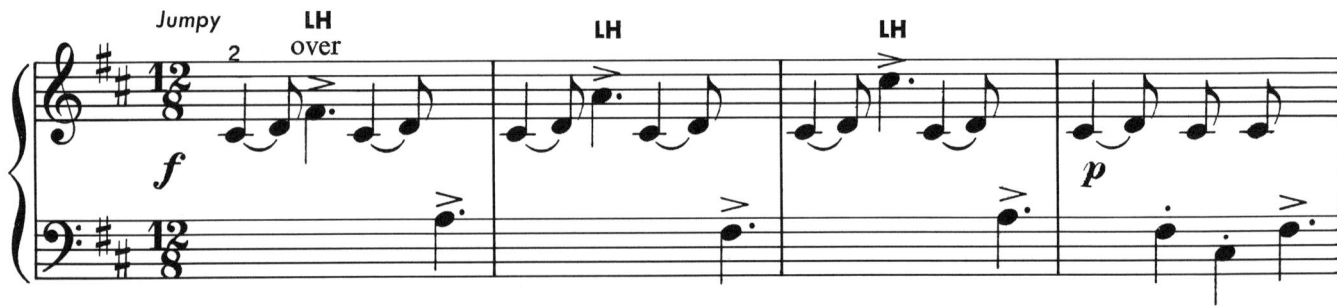

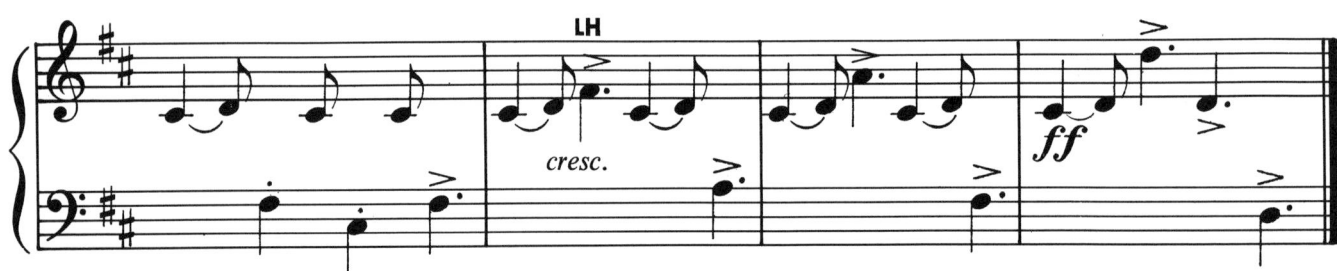

This piece uses only four important notes in D major:

tonic (I) _____   dominant (V) _____   the two black keys _____ _____

Which black key does D major use that G major does not? _____

Since this black key is a half step below tonic, it is the leading tone.

24 Accompanying Melodies in D Major

In D major the tones of the tonic triad are ____ ____ ____ ;

the *non*-tonic tones are ____ ____ ____ ____ .

When you can play each melody easily, make a **LH** accompaniment for it (follow the instructions on page 31).

25 More About Using the Leading Tone in Accompaniments

As you already know, measures made mostly of *non*-tonic tones can be accompanied with dominant (**V**) or leading tone (**LT**).

But when the leading tone occurs *in the melody*, it is *not used in the accompaniment.*

For example:

When you can play each melody easily, make a **LH** accompaniment for it.

1. Mark **V** under measures made mostly of non-tonic tones; then circle the **V** under measures that use **LT** in the melody.

2. Put your **LH** an octave below your **RH**:
    thumb on tonic,
    finger 2 on leading tone,
    finger 4 on dominant.

3. Accompany the melody:
    use dominant where you circled **V**,
    use dominant *or* **LT** where **V** is not circled,
    use tonic everywhere else.

26 Using Important Tones in a Key to Make Music

OPUS 5

Here are three musical ideas, one in each of the keys you have studied so far.

(Notice that each idea uses only the important tones of the key.)

Make each idea into a complete piece, in any way you like.
Use only the important tones in each key.

Clocks is in _____ major. Important notes in this key are:

tonic (I) _____   dominant (V) _____

Copycat is in _____ major. Important notes in this key are:

tonic (I) _____   dominant (V) _____   the only black key _____

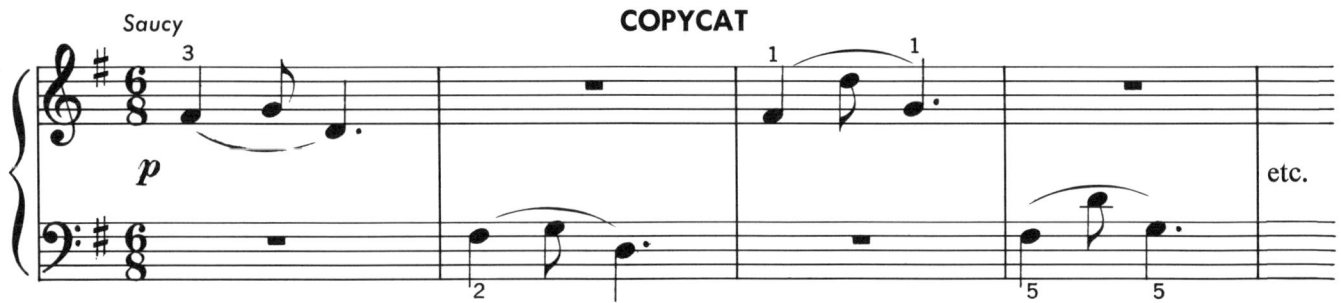

Argument is in _____ major. Important notes in this key are:

tonic (I) _____   dominant (V) _____   the two black keys _____ _____

37

27 Sixteenth Notes*

As you know, a quarter note can be divided into *two* equal parts or *three* equal parts.

A quarter note can also be divided into *four* equal parts, called **sixteenth notes.**

Eighth notes are connected with *one* beam .

Sixteenth notes are connected with *two* beams ( ).

To learn these sixteenth-note rhythms:
1. Point to the notes and count.
2. Tap and count.

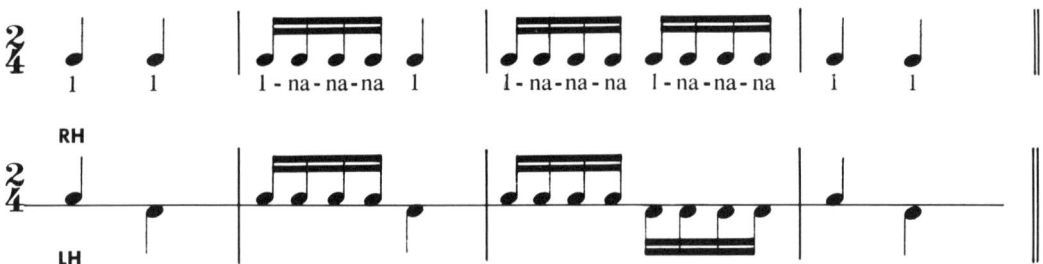

Here are some melodies using sixteenth notes.

Before playing, tap and count.

HURRY

We know *Hurry* is in the key of C major because:

the melody ends on the tonic _____ ;

there are *no* sharps or flats in the key signature.

*See Explanatory Note (page 3) for explanation of counting.

We know *Breathless* is in the key of G major because:

    the melody ends on the tonic _____ ;

    the key signature is one sharp _____ .

In each hand, which finger will play a black key? _____

We know *Ski Jump* is in the key of C major because:

    the melody ends on the tonic _____ ;

    there are _____ sharps or flats in the key signature.

We know *Toe Dancer* is in the key of D major because:

    the melody ends on the tonic _____ ;

    the key signature is two sharps _____ and _____ .

In the music, circle all the notes you will play on black keys.

On the piano, find the F♯'s and C♯'s you will play in this piece.

28 Using Sixteenth Notes to Make Music

Here is a theme you have played before. It is in _____ major.

THEME

You can make another set of variations on this theme by using neighbor tones in ♪♪♪♪ patterns to decorate each **RH** note.
For example:

VARIATION 1

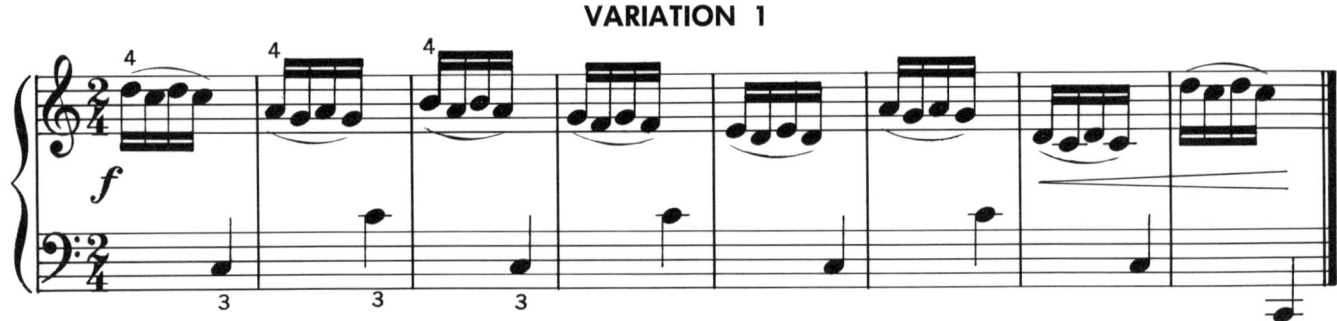

In *Variation 1*, each note is decorated by playing a neighbor tone, the theme tone, a neighbor tone, and finally the theme tone again, using the rhythm ♪♪♪♪

Are the neighbor tones a half step or a whole step *above* the theme tones?   **H   W**

Here are two other ways to decorate this theme.

Complete each variation with the decorating figure given.

VARIATION 2   **VARIATION 3**

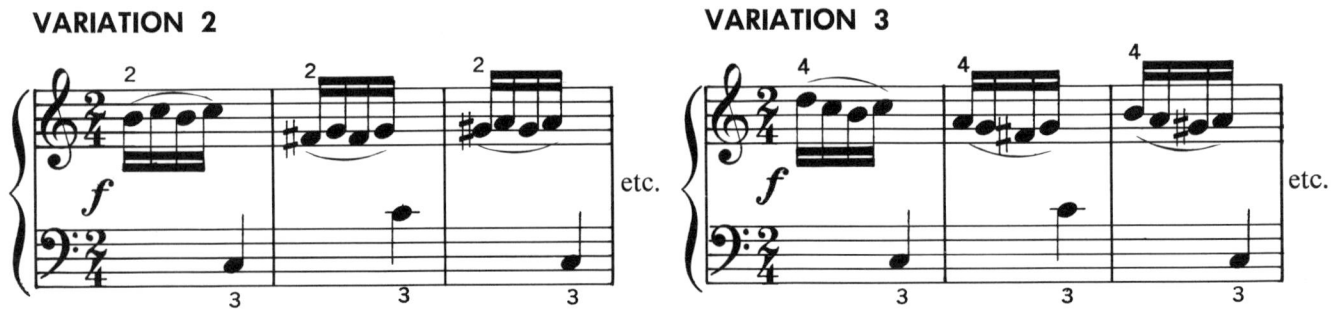

Now play the entire piece — the theme and all three variations.

40

29 Accompanying Melodies that Use Sixteenth Notes

Here are some melodies using sixteenth notes.

Before playing each melody:

1. Circle the notes you will play on black keys.
2. Tap and count the rhythm.

When you can play each melody *easily and securely*, make a **LH** accompaniment for it (follow the instructions on page 36).

30 The Key of F Major

Look back at the experiment on page 29 and study the key of F major.

On this keyboard, mark the keys to complete F major.

F major uses one black key, B♭.

B♭ is the **TOP / BOTTOM** key in the groups of **TWO / THREE** black keys.

F major uses all the white keys in the octave except_____.

Berceuse is in the key of F major. We know it is F major because:

it ends on the tonic_____; the key signature is one flat_____.

In the music, circle all the notes you will play on black keys.

On the piano, find all the B♭'s you will play in this piece.

BERCEUSE

The **LH** of this piece uses only three important notes in the key:

tonic **(I)** _____   dominant **(V)** _____   the only black key _____

The only black key is a half step *above* degree_____. It is degree_____.

42

31 Accompanying Melodies in F Major

In F major the tones of the tonic triad are ____ ____ ____ ;

the *non*-tonic tones are ____ ____ ____ ____ .

When you can play each melody easily, make a **LH** accompaniment for it (follow the instructions on page 36).

32 The Key of B♭ Major

Look back at the experiment on page 29 and study the key of B♭ major.

On this keyboard, mark the keys to complete B♭ major.

B♭ major uses two black keys, B♭ and E♭.

They are the **TOP / BOTTOM** keys in the groups of black keys.

B♭ major uses all the white keys in the octave except ___ and ___.

Procession is in the key of B♭ major. We know it is B♭ major because:

it ends on the tonic ___ ; the key signature is two flats ___ and ___.

In the music, circle all the notes you will play on black keys.

On the piano, find all the B♭'s and E♭'s you will play in this piece.

PROCESSION

The **LH** of this piece uses only four important notes in the key:

tonic (I) ___   dominant (V) ___   the two black keys ___ ___

Which black key does B♭ major use that F major does not? ___

This black key is a half step *above* degree ___. It is degree ___.

33. Accompanying Melodies in B♭ Major

In B♭ major the tones of the tonic triad are ___ ___ ___ ;

the *non*-tonic tones are ___ ___ ___ ___ .

When you can play each melody easily, make a **LH** accompaniment for it (follow the instructions on page 36).

34 Half Note as the Sign for One Pulse

In the music you have played so far, the bottom number of the time signature has always been 4 or 8.

But there are also time signatures in which the bottom number is 2.

In this music 𝅗𝅥 = **one pulse**.

$\frac{2}{2}$ $\frac{3}{2}$

To count this music: for each 𝅗𝅥 say 1

for each 𝅝 say 1 - 2

for each 𝅝. say 1 - 2 - 3

Before playing *Melody,* point to the **RH** notes and count.

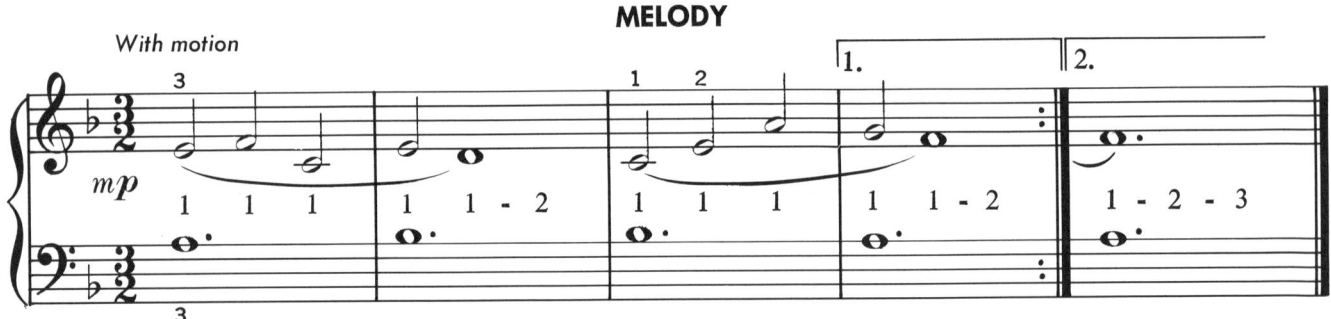

A half-note pulse can be divided into two parts: 𝅗𝅥 = ♩ ♩
                                                      1 - na

or four parts: 𝅗𝅥 = ♫♫
               1 - na - na - na

To learn this new rhythm:

1. Point to the notes and count.
2. Tap and count.

* ¢ is another sign for $\frac{2}{2}$

Here are two pieces you have played before, but this time written with the half note as the sign for one pulse.

Before playing each piece:
1. Look at the key signature and answer the questions.
2. Point to the notes and count.

Ski Jump has the key signature of one flat _____.

Bb is the **TOP / BOTTOM** key in the groups of **TWO / THREE** black keys.

Circle all the Bb's in the music.

Toe Dancer has the key signature of two flats _____ and _____ .

Bb and Eb are the **TOP / BOTTOM** keys in the groups of black keys.

Circle all the Bb's and Eb's in the music.

47

35 Accompanying Melodies When ♩ Is the Sign for One Pulse

When you can play each melody *easily and securely,* make a **LH** accompaniment for it (follow the instructions on page 36).

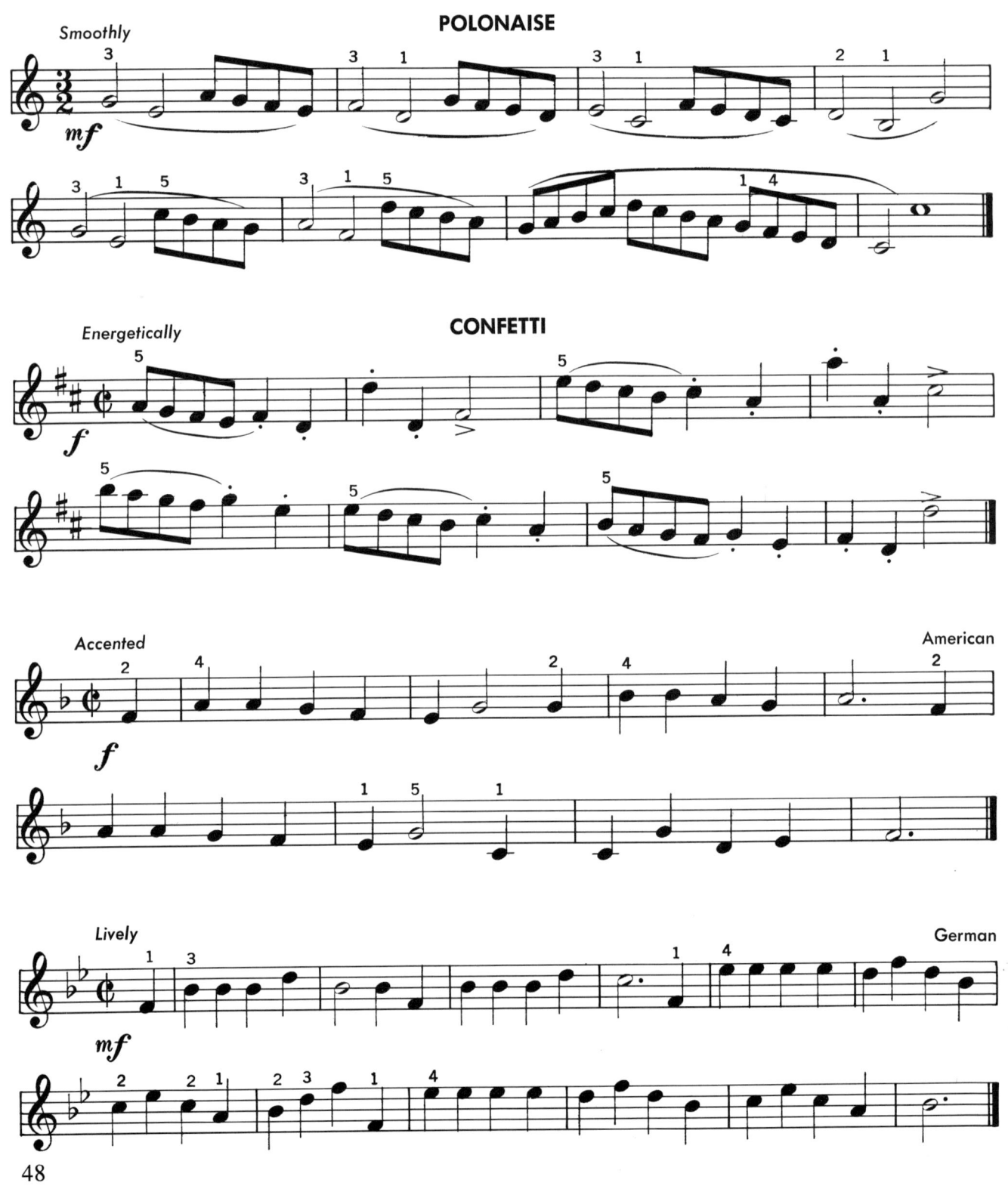